Top Tips

**From the 'Letterbocks'
pages of**

Viz

ISBN 1 870 870 514

Published in Great Britain by
John Brown Publishing Limited,
The Boathouse, Crabtree Lane, Fulham,
London SW6 6LU.

First printing October 1994

Printed in Great Britain and France.
Bound in Great Britain.

TOP TIPS

From the 'Letterbocks' pages of

Viz

Edited by Chris Donald

Written by Chris Donald, Graham Dury,
Simon Thorp, Simon Donald
and the many Viz readers
who have contributed.

Special thanks to
Dave Purnell, Dave Treloar
and 'Hapag Lloyd'.

Illustrations by Davey Jones.

CONTENTS

KITCHEN AND COOKERY

SHOPS AND SHOPPING

HEALTH AND HYGIENE

FASHION AND CLOTHING

SOCIAL AND RECREATIONAL

HOUSEHOLD HINTS 2

HouseHold Hints 1

EMPTY cereal packets make ideal holders for old toilet roll tubes and milk bottle tops which one should never throw away as they are most handy, and have a variety of uses.

Mrs A. Ellis
Wrexham

WHEN reading a book try tearing out the pages as you read them. This saves the expense of buying a bookmark, and the pages can later be used for shopping lists.

Mrs P. Hamilton
Arbroath

WASHING up bottles, once empty, make ideal containers for storing petrol. I always buy a few gallons if I see a special offer anywhere, and keep it under the stairs or on top of my wardrobe.

Mrs S. Gray
Carlisle

READERS with old or perished hot water bottles may, after filling, wish to leave the problem bottle in the sink or bath and so reduce the risk of damp bedclothes.

Mr P. Jopling
Bracknell

WHEN buying toilet tissue I always unwind each roll carefully and number the sheets individually using a Biro or felt-tipped pen.

Mrs Howard
Bingley

MY husband and I save pounds every year on household wear and tear by living in a tent in the garden.

Mrs. I. Stokes
Potters Bar

HANG a Cornflakes packet on a piece of string in all the doorways of your house. Bumping into the brightly coloured boxes as you pass through will remind you to close the door behind you.

Mrs A. Ellis
Wrexham

WEIGH toilet rolls on your kitchen scales and record their weight after each visit to the toilet. On each occasion deduct the new weight from their previous weight. The figure remaining will be the exact weight of toilet tissue which you have used on that particular 'visit'.

Mrs Howard
Bingley

SMELL gas? Locate the suspected leak by striking an ordinary match in every room in the house until a loud explosion reveals the source of the escaping gas.

N. Burke
Manchester

STOP nosey neighbours from knowing which room you're in by stealthily crawling around the house on all fours.

D. E. Blancharde
Fragsthorpe

KEEP a roll of Sellotape handy in the bathroom to stick back any unused pieces of toilet tissue which you pull off the roll by mistake.

D. Page
Burnley

IF you have guests staying overnight, always shave their pillows beforehand. I always do this, and have yet to receive a single complaint about feathers protruding.

Mrs Doris Price
Berkshire

TRAIL a six foot length of toilet tissue along your bathroom floor, over the rim of your lavatory bowl and into the water. Flush the toilet and then watch as the tissue is 'eaten' by the bowl, like someone sucking in spaghetti.

A. Tait
Newcastle

PRETEND you have a fantastic sex life by bouncing up and down on your bed several times a day, moaning loudly. Then look at your neighbours' jealous faces every time you leave the house.

P. Pinto
Edgeware

TEACH children the value of money by bursting their football. They will then have to **work** to earn enough money to buy a replacement.

Mr G. Morgan
Finchley

AMUSE you children by dressing as a clown and performing card tricks over breakfast.

I. Beadle
Dartford

COLLECT empty Cornflakes packets in a spare bedroom or attic space. Count them after five years, then divide the total by 260. This will give you a rough idea of how many packets you get through in a week.

B. Fitzpatrick
Wakefield

DON'T waste money on expensive firelighters. Use potato peelings instead. If they don't ignite at first, leave them in an airing cupboard to dry for a few days.

Mr. Sark
Derby

SAVE on laundry bills by keeping your kids' clothes on next time they have a bath. And get them to play with your dirty dinner dishes instead of the usual bath toys.

Mr D. Porterfield
Bracknell

HAVING trouble with obscene phone callers? Try installing an answering machine, and then not switching it on.

A. Dawson
Liverpool

AVOID wasting hot water by emptying the bath into a series of 'Thermos' flasks and storing it until required again.

Mrs S. Ark
Gwent

AS adverts on the television tell us not to use light switches if we smell gas, I find it useful to always have a candle ready for use in such emergencies.

Mrs D. Bibby
Rugby

PLACE a small table behind your front door in order to avoid bending down to pick up the post.

N. Blackett-Ord
Ashton-under-Lyne

PRETEND you are enjoying a sunny beach holiday by putting sandpaper insoles in your slippers and walking around the house in your underpants, with all the lights turned on.

> David Inch
> Chester-le-Street

DON'T answer your front door. It could be burglars.

> Mr F. Corsair
> Bridgnorth

DON'T waste any money on over-priced toilet fresheners. Simply hang pleasant smelling herbal tea bags over the rim of the loo, and every time you flush, hey presto! Your toilet will fill up with lovely tea.

> A. Asda
> Castleton

INJECT food colouring into the bottom of your toothpaste tube using a hypodermic needle. When the toothpaste begins to appear coloured, you'll know it's time to buy a new tube.

> G. Ducksworth
> Barnsley

CARRY a different vegetable in your pocket each weekday to remind you what day it is. For example: Sunday – a sprout, Monday – a marrow, Tuesday – a turnip, Wednesday... etc.

> I. Tobacco
> Bradford

IMPRESS visitors by sitting on their lap, flicking through an animal book, and making the appropriate animal noise for each picture.

> James Taylor
> Sussex

P.S. This works best if you are under two years old.

WRAP lightbulbs in Sellotape to prevent them from shattering in the event that they should fall out of their bayonet fittings for any reason.

> Walter Hurst
> Hendon

BRIDES! Take no chances on your wedding day. Place marshmallows under your wedding cake to help it withstand any minor earthquakes or tremors.

D. Puttnam
Ryhope

SMOKERS. Wear a golf visor between your nose and top lip to keep your cigarette dry in the shower.

D. Quigley
Rotherham

SMUGGLE whisky out of the house by pouring it down the sink and collecting it in a saucepan under the drainpipe.

Steven Pearlman
Soapdish, Hants.

WHEN carrying a cup of tea from one room to another always add a spoonful of cornflower. This will thicken it up and prevent it from spilling over the rim and onto the carpet.

Mrs E. Davis
Blackpool

HOUSE guests will think your finger nails grow quickly if you cut up a table tennis ball and sprinkle pieces around your bathroom sink every morning.

F. Foster
Froddingham

AVOID dirty finger marks around light switches by fixing an ordinary bathroom soap dish and a glass holder by the side of each switch. Guests can then use the soap, and water from the glass, to wash their hands before touching the switch. Oh, and you'll need a small towel rail too.

Mrs. M. Head
Willenhall

CUT out problem pages before you throw magazines away, and send them to the Samaritans. They will then be able to help if they encounter any similar problems themselves.

S. Coulkton
Sefton

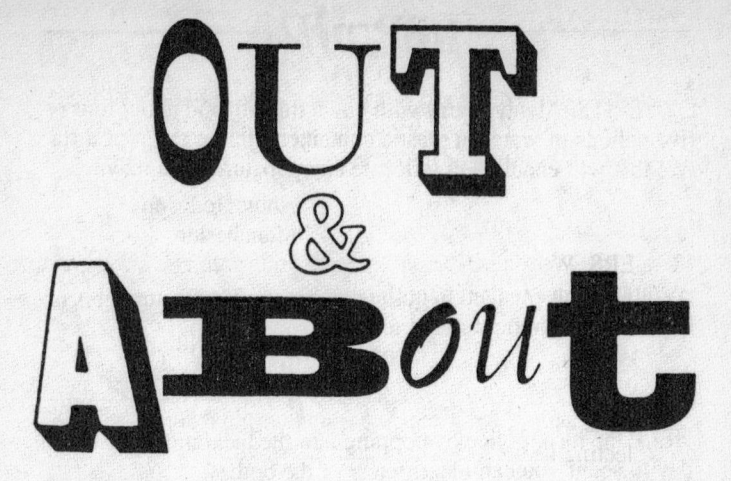

OUT & About

AVOID embarrassment after tripping in the street by repeating the same movement several times to make it seem like part of your normal behaviour.

B. Sweeny
Cove Road

SAVE time when crossing a one-way street by only looking in the direction of oncoming traffic.

D. Rogers
Hemel Hempstead

EVERY day make a list of everything you do, and hand it in at your local police station. That way you can be eliminated from their enquiries in the event of a crime.

D. Anon
Monkchester

WHEN boarding a bus routinely try to avoid paying your fare by claiming you are with the person in front of you.

I. Peters
Gravesend

WHEN crossing a one-way street, always look in **both** directions in case a large, blue furniture removal lorry is reversing the wrong way up the road.

D. Rogers
Hemel Hempstead
General Infirmary

CYCLISTS. Always carry with you a tin bath and about four or five gallons of water in plastic containers. In the event of a flat tyre this will enable you to locate any punctures you may have.

Andy Hodgson
Manchester

AVOID being engaged in polite conversations with strangers on buses by pretending to be drunk.

Trevor Williams
Woolwich

HELP the local police by popping into the local mortuary every day to see if you can identify any of the bodies.

J. Lewis
Lichfield

NEXT time you're at the seaside try turning your greenhouse upside down and fitting an outboard motor. The kids will be kept occupied for hours watching the fascinating underwater flora and colourful fish.

M. Thresher
Bristol

BEAT the credit card companies at their own game by running up massive bills on your credit cards and then killing yourself before your statements arrive, thus avoiding re-payment.

D. Payne
Middlesex

PRETEND you're a German on holiday by being rude to your neighbours, over eating at breakfast time, and barging into the queue at the post office.

T. Pearson
Hull

CITY gents. Simulate the thrills of ski jumping by leaning forward and placing your umbrella under your arm next time you go down an escalator.

Matty
Liverpool

CONVINCE friends you've joined the Socialist Workers' Party by becoming unsociable, giving up work, and standing on street corners ranting away on subjects about which you know very little.

Karl Lyall
Carlisle

WHEN dining in restaurants don't start eating until every course has been brought to the table. With your whole order laid out in front of you it is much easier to check the bill when it arrives.

F. Consul
Leeds

AVOID being mugged in the street by walking along behind a policeman, moving your lips and gesturing as if you are engaged in a friendly conversation with him. If he turns round simply look confused, and ask him for directions to a nearby street.

R. Hollins
Hammersmith

AVOID paying tax by going to work in a politically unstable Middle East country inhabited by religious fanatics. Ignore British Government advice to leave when a war looks imminent, then moan a few weeks later when bombs start going off and there aren't any planes home.

S. Goblin
Middlesex

TAKE a lead out of the skateboarders' book this winter. Strap egg cartons to your knees and elbows to prevent injury when falling on icy pavements.

G. Hall
Motherwell

WHEN it stops raining run to the nearest car park. By counting the number of dry patches you can work out how many cars have left the car park since the rain stopped.

H. Dingle
London

SIMILARLY by looking underneath all the cars and counting the number of vehicles with wet tarmac below them you can work out how many cars have arrived since the rain stopped.

H. Dingle
London

THE TOTAL of the two figures represents the net traffic flow through the car park's 'Entrance/Exit' in the moments since precipitation ceased.

H. Dingle
London

UNFORTUNATELY any car which arrived after the rain stopped, and parked on a recently vacated dry space, would not be accountable by this method.

H. Dingle
London

TREAT yourself on birthdays or other special occasions by carrying your favourite comfortable chair around with you everywhere you go. When you get tired of carrying the chair you can sit down in it and give yourself a well earned rest.

Gary Bennett
Oxford

PRETEND you don't live in Tottenham by walking around Tottenham with an A to Z guide asking people for directions.

Simone Glover
Tottenham

FOIL pick pockets by placing a freshly toasted 'Pop Tart' in each pocket. Would-be thieves will quickly rupture the fragile pastry and receive nasty finger burns from the steaming hot jam inside.

P. Turner
Liverpool L17

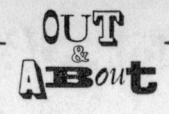

ALWAYS keep a pound of lard in your pocket so that if you get your head stuck in railings you'll be able to grease your ears and slide out.

Kate Emblen
Uxbridge

SAVE money on expensive nicotine gum by chewing ordinary gum and smoking a cigarette at the same time.

H. Cavendar
Kingston

ALWAYS carry a five pence piece in your pocket so that if you fancy a Chinese takeaway you can buy a plastic fork.

H. Attwell
Enfield

WHEN holidaying abroad include a toilet brush and standard lamp in your luggage. Hotels rarely provide toilet brushes, and the lamp will come in handy for reading.

Mrs. D. Patterson
Shrewsbury

SPECTACLE wearers. Stand at your local car wash on Sunday mornings and ask successive drivers if they'd mind hanging your glasses from their radiator grille while they wash their car.

R. M.
Southampton

A BLACK bin liner draped over a TV aerial makes a cheap yet effective umbrella, particularly handy in the wet and blustery spring months.

D. Topper
Woking

FINE tune your eye/hand co-ordination by trying to 'bomb' ants or similar crawling insects on the pavement on your way to work, using small ball bearings. Every day increase precision by using a smaller size ball bearing.

Tim Erroll
Romford

MUFFLE the sound of your Walkman to prevent it annoying others by placing a tea bag between your headphones and each ear.

A. Asda
Castleford

FELLAS. Whenever you visit a pub with a male friend wear a passport sized photograph of your wife, cut into the shape of a heart, on your lapel in order to dispel any rumours that you might be homosexual.

L. Hall
Newcastle

SAVE money on expensive tickets to 'open air festivals' next summer. Simply put up a tent in your own back garden, piss up the side of it, and steal your own shoes.

Simone Glover
Tottenham N15

Motoring & Travel

PRESSING the middle pedal in my car helps me to slow down when approaching busy junctions or built up areas.

> Mr G. Lane
> Hartburn, Cleveland

MAKE your car much easier to find in a large car park by letting down all the tyres. On your return simply look for the lowest car.

> Bill Norman
> Cardiff

MAKE your car look like a taxi (from a considerable distance) by Sellotaping a Cornflakes packet to the roof.

> A. Gallagher
> Runcorn

SAVE petrol by pushing your car to your destination. Invariably passers-by will think you've broken down and help.

> S. Pate
> Glasgow

SAVE having to buy expensive personalised number plates by simply changing your name to match your existing plate.

> Mr. KVL 741Y
> Lincoln

PUT a stop to car thieves by syphoning off all your petrol whenever you park your car, and carrying it round with you in one or two plastic buckets.

D. Griffiths
Kent

MOTORCYCLISTS. Save cigarette filters and stick them up your nostrils. These will prevent dirt getting in, whilst still allowing you to breathe.

S. Pissuillie
Mackay, Australia

KEEP a tin of red paint handy in your car. If you see an accident you can quickly pour it over yourself and pretend to be involved.

J. Mitchell
Southampton

PREVENT sneak thieves from stealing the crook lock from your car by attaching one end to the steering wheel and the other to one of the floor pedals.

D. Marshall (Mr)
Stockton-on-Tees

WHEN out driving always turn left. Then, should you become lost, you can find your way home by reversing the procedure and always turning right.

Mr. B.M.W. Five-Series
Aldershot

CAR thieves. Always carry a spare can of petrol with you in case the driver has syphoned off all the petrol from his car and is carrying it round with him in one or two plastic buckets.

A. Thief
Kent

DON'T risk drowning next time you travel by boat. Simply wear a pair of bicycle clips and fill your trousers with ping-pong balls.

A. Clayton
Glasgow

A FEW drops of car engine oil mixed with treacle will help it flow more easily from the tin. I would imagine.

Dave Moore
Nottingham

AVOID being wheel clamped by jacking your car up, removing the wheels and locking them safely in the boot till you return.

Angus Carr
Oxfordshire

FOOL neighbours into thinking your car has an expensive alarm fitted by sleeping in it every night, turning your hazard lights on and constantly sounding the horn at regular intervals.

M. Planck
Stafford

RE-SPRAYING your car? Cover it with 'Cling Film' first. If you don't like the new colour, simply peel it off and start again.

Denise Jordan
Petts Wood

FOOL other drivers into thinking you have an expensive car phone by holding an old TV or video remote control up to your ear and occasionally swerving across the road and mounting the kerb.

Mike Penny
Coventry

PAINT the windows of your car black to enjoy the benefits of night-time driving during the day.

P. Murray
Hampstead

AVOID jetlag on foreign trips by simply taking an earlier flight, thus arriving fully refreshed and on time.

Sgt. R. J. Crowe
662 Squadron, Germany

KEEP the seat next to you on the train vacant by smiling and nodding at people as they walk up the aisle.

Mrs Deidre Partridge
Rugby

ANNOY traffic wardens by knocking their hats off.

Mr I. Woods
Bolton

CONVINCE neighbours that you have an expensive alarm by locking your car and then making loud, high pitched 'whooping' noises as you walk away.

S. Black
Burnley

HOUSEWIVES. When driving to the shops always carry a stiff broom in the boot of your car. Use it to sweep the broken glass to the side of the road every time you have a minor accident.

D. Stammers
Canvey Island

IMAGINE you're in London by simply sitting in your car all day with the engine running, occasionally honking your horn, and never actually going anywhere.

G. Foster
Blyth

KEEP a foot pump next to your brake pedal, and connect it to an inflatable paddling pool folded on your lap. If you are about to crash, pump rapidly and the inflated pool will cushion you from injury.

J. Thompson
Prestwick

PARKING problems? Tie a balloon to the front bumper of your car, and Sellotape a drawing pin to the rear wall of your garage. When you hear the balloon burst, apply the brakes.

Q. Quicksave
Quebec

CYCLISTS. Avoid getting flies in your eyes by making an improvised pair of goggles out of two tea strainers.

> P. Presto
> Preston

CENTRALLY position your car within your garage by fixing a torch to the exact centre of the bonnet. Then line up the beam with a target placed on the centre of the rear wall (above the drawing pin). Then drive slowly forwards aiming the beam at the target (until the balloon bursts).

> Q. Quicksave
> Quebec

LOOK 'hard' on train journeys by saving up all your empty beer cans for a month and then lining them up on the table in front of you.

> Tugger Trotman
> Wirral

ATTACH a Christmas cracker by two pieces of string, one to your front bumper and one to your garage wall, the total length being equal to that of your garage. Then reverse your car out the garage. When the cracker explodes, stop, get out of the car, and close the garage door.

> Q. Quicksave
> Quebec

RAILWAY commuters. When boarding your train attach a length of rope to the carriage door, and tie the other end firmly around your ankle. In the event of a crash you will be able to find your way out of the wreckage by simply following the rope.

> Dave Parsnip
> Altrincham

WHEN travelling by train jot down a note of any refreshments you require and pin it to your lapel. This will save you having to talk to the miserable bastard who is invariably serving in the buffet car.

> P. Donnelly
> Portsmouth

LEAVE your headlights on whenever you park your car in a large car park. If you are unable to find it on your return, simply go away again and come back when it has got dark.

M. Ross
Peckham

BEAT police speed traps by stopping your car every 200 yards and pretending to mess around under the bonnet. This way traffic cops will be unable to accurately record your speed for any length of time.

S. Daniels
Halifax

WHEN parking in car parks always carry a spare battery in the boot of your car in case the other one has gone flat by the time you eventually find your car.

M. Ross
Peckham

GIRLS. Practice being an air hostess by standing up at the end of the aisle and demonstrating emergency landing procedures every time you get on a bus.

Mrs Joyce Clooney
Littlehampton

FOOL onlookers into believing your car has central locking by leaving all the doors unlocked except the driver's door. When you return open the driver's door and – hey presto! All the doors are suddenly unlocked.

Tom Bradley
Heaton

BUS drivers. Pretend you're an airline pilot by wedging your accelerator peddle down with a heavy book, securing the steering wheel with some old rope, and then strolling back along your bus chatting casually to the passengers.

Mrs Joyce Clooney
Littlehampton

CYCLISTS. Why not try stopping at red lights like everyone else, instead of riding up onto the pavement to avoid them. Stupid bastards.

> M. Burridge
> Newcastle

PENSIONERS. Try sitting on a pile of encyclopedias next time you go for a drive in your car. That way you'll be able to see out of the front window.

> B. Flynn
> Burnley

AND while you're on, try pushing the pedal on the right down towards the floor. That will make your car move forwards more quickly.

> B. Flynn
> Burnley

POLICE. Get prime seats for your local panto this year by stopping one of the stars as they drive home after the show full of drink. They're bound to offer you free tickets.

> P. Noble
> Torquay

MOTORISTS. Pressing your 'fog lights' switch a second time after the fog has cleared will actually turn the fog lights off.

> J.C.
> Luton

A TEASPOON placed in a glass on the back seat of your car makes a handy audible gauge for road bump severity.

> R. Crabb
> Nantwich

WHEN travelling by bus always take a polaroid photo of the queue so that when the bus arrives any arguments about people 'pushing in' can easily be settled.

> R. Holmes
> Putney

FOIL fiddling taxi drivers by taking polaroid photographs of street signs you pass them. At the end of the journey you can confront him with photographic evidence if he has taken an unnecessarily long route.

R. Holmes
Putney

BEAT bicycle theft by towing a horse box behind your bike. When you stop, simply padlock the cycle securely inside the horse box.

Don Brayford
Withersfield, Suffolk

TAXI drivers. Why not pop into the garage and ask them to fix your indicator lights for you so that other motorists know where the fuck you are going.

E. Murphy
Ipswich

DRINK drivers. Before motoring home after an evening on the piss, try sucking on an extra strong mint. Later, when police stop you for swerving around in the middle of the road and failing to stop at a red light, they'll never in a million years suspect you've been drinking.

R. Luck
H.M. Prison, Shotts.

WHEN on the continent simplify the process of driving on the 'wrong side' of the road by placing your rear view mirror above your back windscreen. Then simply look over your shoulder whilst driving and view the road ahead in the re-positioned mirror. Everything will appear perfectly normal, with cars driving on the 'left' side of the road.

J. Sulzer
Ipswich

A LARGE sheet of polystyrene placed on your car roof and trimmed to shape makes an ideal 'all weather' snow covering with which to baffle fellow motorists in summer.

Steve Murphy
Gloucester

AVOID peak hour congestion between Stirling and Glasgow at the A80 Auchinkilns roundabout by taking the A8011 through Cumbernauld and rejoining the A80 beyond this bottleneck.

G. Keddie
Glasgow

STUDENTS. On trains why not dump your rucksack on the seat next to you instead of the luggage rack provided. This will ensure that taxpayers have to stand throughout their journey while you sit back in your subsidised seat, talking loudly.

Eric Hoggers
Hayes, Middlesex

WINTER is the time to freeze petrol and store it in the ice tray of your fridge. Come summer these handy 'petrol cubes' will help to cool your engine as you drive along.

B. Baxter
Potters Bar

AVOID parking tickets by leaving your windscreen wipers turned on to 'fast wipe' whenever you leave your car parked illegally.

S. Tyler
Norwich

MAKE firelighters by steeping white nougat overnight in your petrol tank.

B. Baxter
Potters Bar

IF THE driver behind is too close, simply pull on the handbrake. This will not activate your brakelights, and he will have no warning that you are about to stop. Watch his face in your rear view mirror as his car slams into the back of you.

D. Campbell
Cambridge
(not the university)

REMOVE your trousers and tie them around your neck before you get into your car. You will then be able to remove your handkerchief, keys or wallet from your trouser pocket with ease, even after you have fastened your seat belt.

> J. Varley
> London N18

LADIES. When commuting to work try leaving the house five minutes earlier than usual in order that male commuters may be spared the ridiculous spectacle of you trying to 'run' for a train.

> Eric Hoggers
> Hayes, Middlesex

GAUGE local night-time wind conditions by installing an ultra sensitive alarm in your soft top sports car. The most moderate of gusts will activate the alarm and keep both yourself and your neighbours fully informed as to local wind conditions.

> M. Retard
> Cambridge

WOMEN drivers. When driving to work try getting out of bed ten minutes earlier than usual. This will enable you to put your make-up on using the bathroom mirror, and not in the rear view mirror of your car whilst sitting at a green traffic light.

> A. Compass
> Red Leceistershire

DON'T waste electricity flashing your headlights to invite buses to pull out in front of you. They invariably do so anyway.

> H. Attwell
> Enfield

NEXT time you fill your tyres with air at the garage charge the attendant 10p for each breath you take while you're talking to him.

> D. Thompson
> Wivenhoe

HOME AND GARDEN

A HANDY gardening tip I learnt from my father is to build a fence or wall inbetween your garden and that of your neighbour. This wall or fence then provides an invaluable indication of where your garden ends and your neighbour's begins.

A. P.
Bridlington

I FILLED the rectangular hole at the front of my house with a wooden door. As well as reducing heat loss, my 'door' is also a deterrent to would-be burglars.

A. Tenanty
Sheffield

ENLARGE your living space by removing that bulky light shade and gluing sea shells directly onto the bulb.

Doris Pratt
Billingham

SOIL lasts longer if you dip it in vinegar first.

D. Johnson
Leeds

PRETEND your house is a 'Bed and Breakfast' establishment by ordering an extra ten pints of milk each day, and placing a 'Bed and Breakfast' sign in your front window. Unwanted callers can be dissuaded by adding a simple 'No Vacancies' sign.

A. Conway
Dundee

DISCOURAGE burglars by wearing a policeman's uniform and standing outside your house day and night.

> G. Byker
> Rotherhyde

GARDENERS. Save money during the summer months by plugging your electrical lawn mower into your next door neighbour's electricity supply.

> R. Hope
> Timperley

MAKE polystyrene life belts for your plant pots and float your house plants in the bath when you go on holiday.

> D. Price
> Bradford

INCREASE the size of your garden by moving the fence several feet into your neighbour's garden during the night.

> R. Hope
> Timperley

DON'T throw away that left-over paint. Turn your garden into a helicopter landing pad by painting a large 'H' in the middle of the lawn, using white emulsion and a roller.

> Paul Sweeney
> Kirkham

TURN your greenhouse into a garden shed by boarding up the windows with spare floorboards.

> S. T.
> Pontefract

NEXT time you decorate put wallpaper up with 'Blu-Tac' It's much less messy, and expensive wallpaper can then be taken with you when you move house.

> E. McAndrews
> Didsbury

MAKE neighbours think you've had a house fire by blackening your windows with shoe polish and throwing your mattresses out into the garden.

F. Lee
Manchester

SAVE money on batteries by making your own novel doorbell. Simply thread some empty beer cans on a piece of string and hang them from the front door. Visitors can rattle them to attract your attention.

A. Soreskin
Swindon

MAKE your neighbour think you're an alien by wrapping yourself from head to foot in tinfoil and standing in your garden late at night pointing at the stars, and making silly, high-pitched 'bleeping' noises.

Mrs B. Mirellees
March

DIVIDE your lawn into a grid using string and wooden pegs. You can then describe your exact position in the garden over the phone to a friend or relative many miles away who would then be able to plot your movements on a piece of graph paper.

R. H. Lorimer
Peebles

KEEP your insurance company on their toes by ringing them to say that your roof has just blown off in a storm, then calling back ten minutes later to say that you were mistaken.

I. Battenburg
Walsall

ATTACH a tag bearing your name and address to your house keys. If they are lost whoever finds them can then return them to you. On the back of the tag list the times when your house is empty, so that they'll be sure to catch you when they call.

P. Pegley
Hammersmith

DON'T sell that old car for scrap. Park it outside your house, remove the engine and fill the gap with soil and flowers. Hey presto! An instant garden.

Dave Mullahey
Liverpool

UNEMPLOYED? Annoy your neighbour by sprinkling nettle and other weed seeds into his flower beds while he's at work.

Stef Miller
Sheffield

CUT a kitchen chair in half, nail an old floorboard between the two pieces and you have a cheap and attractive garden bench.

A. Harmer
Frodsham

I FIND that an empty Cornflakes box filled with small stones or pebbles makes an ideal paperweight, or handy doorstopper.

Mrs M.
Liverpool

SAVE yourself the trouble of re-potting houseplants by putting them in a big enough pot in the first place.

P. Manderville
Marlborough

CREATE a perfect pond for small gardens by burying an old saucepan and filling it with water. Add an upturned soda syphon and hey presto! An ornamental fountain.

G. Wilmot
Edmundbyers

CONVINCE neighbours and any passers-by that you have fluorescent strip lights in your bedroom by rapidly flicking the switch on and off for a few moments every evening before you enter the room.

Mike Millar
Glasgow

I'D imagine that shorter, thinner lengths of wire connecting appliances to the mains will probably reduce the amount of electricity they use.

Peter Redman
Devizes

FOOL dinner guests into thinking you have woodworm in the house by drilling small holes in the arms and legs of your dining chairs.

S. Cooper
Tring

EDGE your lawn into the shape of a pair of trousers, then mow it in lines so that from above it looks like a giant pair of corduroy pants. Pockets can easily be added by planting small flower beds.

Hapag Lloyd
Runcorn

PRETEND you have dry rot by filling your sub floor void with candy floss.

S. Cooper
Tring

GIVE your bird box that 'thatched cottage' look by fixing two Shredded Wheat to the roof.

A. E. Greenall
Liverpool L11

CON passing aeroplane passengers into thinking your house has an outdoor swimming pool by painting a large blue rectangle on your lawn.

Mr Paul
Crawley

OBTAIN the appearance of mice infestation by making small holes in your skirting boards and scattering a few currants around the floor.

S. Cooper
Tring

GARDENERS. Take a tip from fashion designers. Paint long, thin parallel lines on your garden hose to give the impression that it is longer than it actually is. Or paint thicker hoops along its length to create a new, shorter look.

> Percy Bike
> Huddersfield

OBTAIN the effects of satellite TV by nailing a dustbin lid to the front of your house, then filling an old fish tank with shit and sitting, staring at it for 23 hours a day.

> J. Brush
> Loughborough

TOE NAIL clippings, chopped up finely, make an ideal substitute for wood chippings when repairing wood chip wallpaper.

> T. Marriage
> Fulham

SLOW traffic down in your street by getting your wife to dress as a policewoman and stand pointing a hairdryer at cars as they pass by.

> R. Nest
> Chippenham

TRANSFORM your garden into a 'EuroDisney' style theme park by charging your neighbour £20 to get in, £5 for an ice cream, and then making him wait four hours for a ride on your lawn mower.

> S. Tempest
> Plymouth

MARRIED couples. Find out where you live in relation to other buildings in the neighbourhood by driving to a nearby hill while your 'other half' lets off an emergency flare from a bedroom window.

> R. Worsnop
> Chesterfield

FEEL like a million dollars next time you arrive home by gluing Rice Krispies onto your car tyres. When you park it will sound as if you are rolling up on an expensive gravel drive.

> D. Treloar
> Wandsworth

TRANSFORM your garage into an American style 'drive-in' restaurant by sitting in your car, lowering your window and demanding that your wife brings you a cup of tea, on roller skates.

> S. Safeway
> Surbiton

AVOID backache from bending to pick your tomatoes. Simply dig a trench four feet deep alongside your plants. Step into the trench and you'll find your tomatoes are conveniently at chest height.

> John Tagliarini
> Sicily

Kitchen and Cookery

A LARGE pot of home-made soup is an inexpensive way to feed the family. Make it last longer by eating it with forks.

Mrs K. Littlewood
Evesham

I FIND that two lightly buttered pieces of bread put together with a piece of cheese inbetween makes an exciting lunchtime snack. This tasty treat is now a regular in my household. My wife Jean calls it 'Jack's Cheese and Bread Snack'.

Mr J. Pewty
Leeds

WHEN arranging kitchen furniture avoid placing tables or cupboards directly in front of a fridge or oven as they may prevent the fridge or oven doors from opening properly.

T. Barlow
Chester

IT seems such a waste to throw away old toothbrushes. So when one wears out I nip downstairs to the kitchen and pop it inside the Cornflakes box. The following morning it makes a great surprise for the kids.

Mrs D. Partington
Clifton

STOP bread from drying out by keeping it in a bucket of water.

P. J. Ruddock
London

PUT your microwave oven on a shelf **inside** your freezer. That way it will be able to freeze food as well as heat it up.

> Mrs D. Pillage
> Burton-on-Trent

ONE way of keeping hot cooked sausages safe from children is by putting your hot cooked sausages on a work surface and fixing them down with brightly coloured sticky tape.

> Mrs E. Bosomworth
> London

LEAVE one curtain open for every pint of milk you require in the morning.

> Austin Cambridge
> Southwick

WHEN having grandmother or other elderly relatives cremated, always ask the undertaker for their false teeth. These make excellent pastry cutters, and the decorative crust of a pork pie can evoke many happy memories of your loved one.

> A. Richardson
> Carlisle

SAVE time when making a cup of tea by pre-heating the water in a saucepan before putting it in the kettle.

> Susan Craven
> Leeds

WHENEVER you introduce a new system for ordering milk, make sure you explain it to the milkman beforehand.

> Austin Cambridge
> Southwick

TRY painting a red cross at the bottom of tea cups. When this becomes visible your cup will be empty and you may wish to consider a refill.

> Mrs I. Docherty
> Carlisle

WHEN reaching down to pick up dropped cutlery beneath the kitchen table I always wear my husband's motorcycle crash helmet as I invariably bump my head on the table whilst getting up again.

> N. Coquet (Mrs)
> Surrey

WHEN cooking bacon I wear my husband's welding mask and leather apron to protect myself from the spitting fat.

> N. Coquet (Mrs)
> Surrey

ADD beer to washing-up liquid to change it from lemon flavour to shandy flavour.

> Dave Patterson
> Bournemouth

THICKEN up runny low-fat yoghurt by stirring in a spoonful of lard.

> P. Raker
> Chatham

I WEAR my husband's safety boots with steel toe caps when removing tea bags from a cup, as they invariably drip hot water.

> N. Coquet (Mrs)
> Surrey

AVOID over ordering milk by placing your fridge on the pavement just outside your gate. The milkman can then check your day-to-day requirement for himself.

> Phillip Torr
> Essex

POP a few tea bags into your hot water tank and you can make a hot cuppa anytime by simply turning on the hot tap.

> Mrs M. Growitt
> Birmingham

STAND your cooker on an old tea chest. This prevents young children reaching the hot areas, and provides useful storage space for kitchen cleaning equipment, Domestos etc.

Curly Lox
Glastonbury

USE talcum powder on cakes instead of icing sugar. It's a lot cheaper, and much kinder to teeth.

Miss J. Holland
Southfields

FILL a Shredded Wheat with pink soap and hey presto! An inexpensive 'Brillo pad'.

Mrs B. Parkinson
Harrow

CONFUSE your milkman by ordering one pint of milk each day, then buying a dozen extra pints from a nearby shop, thus leaving thirteen empty bottles on the doorstep the following morning. Add to his confusion by leaving a lighted candle in every other bottle.

Mrs P. Wilkinson
Hemel Hempstead

DON'T throw away disposable razors. Keep them in the kitchen. They're ideal for peeling potatoes.

P. J. Ruddock
Nottingham

DRILL a one inch diameter hole in your refrigerator door. This will allow you to check that the light goes off when the door is closed.

T. Baccus
Cheltenham

DON'T throw away used matches. Sharpened with a pen knife, they are ideal for picking up small pieces of cheese, pineapple or cocktail sausages.

S. Jones
Edinburgh

AMAZE your family by secretly making a pretend candle out of a banana, adding an almond at the top for a flame. Then watch their faces as you eat it!

T. Atack
Pontefract

A WIRE paperclip, carefully unfolded, is ideal for picking up small pieces of cheese, pineapple or cocktail sausages.

S. Jones
Edinburgh

DON'T put washing-up liquid in the garage or loft. Keep it handy in the kitchen. I put mine in the cupboard under the sink.

L. Bowman
Tulsa

MAKE the postman think you've had a nose bleed by opening the door with tomato ketchup smeared on your top lip.

Patrick Thistle
Partick Thistle

PREVENT eggs from rolling off kitchen work surfaces by placing them on a small dollop of black treacle.

L. Bowman
Tijuana

DON'T waste a fortune on expensive oven gloves. Boxing gloves, available from most sports shops, will do the job just as well.

M. Cartwright
Borth

MAKE the postman think you have a severe dental abscess by opening the door with a hard-boiled egg secreted in your cheek.

Patrick Thistle
Partick Thistle

DAB a series of dots onto bourbon biscuits with icing, and voila! Edible dominoes.

B. Thompson
Houston

MAKE the postman think you have been sick by opening the door with diced carrots, rice pudding and parmesan cheese smeared down the front of your shirt.

Patrick Thistle
Partick Thistle

POOR people. Can't afford smoked salmon? Simply eat the rubber off an old table tennis bat.

I. Morris
Tiverton

FREEZE loaves of bread, then sculpt them into animal shapes using a hammer and chisel. Once they've thawed, hey presto! Tasty animal bread zoo figures for the kids.

Mrs J. Crooks
Grantham

CUT along one edge of a tea bag and empty out the contents to make an ideal After Eight mint cosy.

A. Asda
Castleford

MAKE mealtimes fun by dipping potatoes in food colouring before slicing and frying. Hey presto! Rainbow chips.

Mrs J. Crookes
Grantham

MAKE your own tea bags by pouring tea into an After Eight mint envelope, and then stapling it closed along the top edge, before puncturing the sides two thousand times with a pin.

A. Asda
Castleford

MAKE edible jumpers for gingerbread men by simply 'knitting' spaghetti with chop sticks.

Mrs L.H.
Longhorsely

CREATE your own 'boil-in-the-bag' cod in parsley sauce by scraping the breadcrumbs off a fish finger and placing it inside a used condom.

E. Evans
Evesham

HOLLOWED out ravioli shells make ideal mittens for gingerbread men.

Mrs L.H.
Longhorsley

DON'T throw away left-over chips. Pop them in a shoebox inside the freezer. Six months later heat them up in the microwave. Hey presto! Exciting American-style french fries.

Mrs Daisy Pengelly
Redruth

WHEN boiling an egg in the morning save time by popping a tea bag and a drop of milk into the saucepan. Hey presto! A boiled egg and a ready-made cup of tea.

Hapag Lloyd
Runcorn

TWO spaghetti hoops make an ideal pair of reading glasses for gingerbread men.

Mrs L.H.
Longhorsely

REMOVE the small plastic beads from cheap necklaces and slip them into your kids' food. You'll then be able to easily identify their stools at a later date, should the need to do so arise.

E. Reid
Ely

SNIP the tails off several hundred small tadpoles using nail scissors to make a tasty (and cheap) caviare substitute.

D. Tanby
Formby

TWO pieces of macaroni stuck together would make an ideal pair of binoculars for any little gingerbread men who express an interest in ornithology.

Mrs L.H.
Longhorsely

BRIGHTEN up breakfast-time by making your toast into simple but effective 'Maltese Cross' shapes by nibbling out an identical section from each of the four corners.

J. Hudson
Mitcham

AVOID cut fingers when chopping vegetables by getting someone else to hold the vegetables for you while you simply chop away.

I. J. Alexander
Birmingham

APPLY first aid to injured gingerbread men by dressing any cuts or scrapes in tagliatelle bandages.

Mrs L.H.
Longhorsely

VARNISH digestive biscuits to make attractive if not slightly brittle drink coasters.

B. Thompson
Houston

SAVE electricity on freezing winter nights by unplugging your fridge and placing the contents on your doorstep.

L. Lipton
Lanarkshire

SINGLE mothers. A life-sized cut-out of Cecil Parkinson in your kitchen will act as an ideal male role model for your disadvantaged children.

R. On
Harringay

LIE Jacob's cream crackers on a 'mattress' consisting of two slices of processed cheese wrapped in kitchen paper, before buttering. This will help to distribute pressure evenly across the back of the biscuit, and prevent cracking.

Hapag Lloyd
Runcorn

PREVENT cats from eating the contents of your fridge while they are standing on your doorstep by surrounding them with chicken wire.

L. Lipton
Lanarkshire

AN old television, with a toaster inside, makes a cheap but effective 'microwave' oven. For making toast.

W. M. Low
Lowick

SHOPS and SHOPPING

ALWAYS buy Cornflakes packets in twos so that you can use one to top the other one up should the contents have settled during transit.

D. Purnell
Bristol

RATHER than carry shopping bags around with me or pay for expensive supermarket carrier bags, I always eat my groceries at the checkout. Not only does this save pounds on carriers, but it has also reduced my gas bill.

Mrs Anne Brookes
Warrington

SHOPKEEPERS. Reduce shoplifting by banning third rate television celebrities from your shop.

A. Price
Worthing

WHEN shopping for shoes I always write my shoe size on a small piece of paper and tuck it into the top of my sock. This saves me having to remove one of my shoes every time I go into a shop.

Mrs F. Tilbrook
Dunstable

BUY onions instead of apples. They are always much cheaper.

Mrs A. Osborne
London

HOUSEWIVES. I find the best way to get two bottles of washing-up liquid for the price of one is by putting one in your shopping trolley and the other in your coat pocket.

Mrs Smith
Chester

WHEN using cash dispensing machines it is possible to prevent the person behind you from knowing your number by deliberately keying in the wrong one. Then pretend to collect your money, and walk away smiling innocently.

A. Walker
Nottingham

WHILE out shopping remove the batteries from any clocks or other battery-operated appliances around the house, and replace them when you return home. This will result in a considerable saving in electricity over a long period of time.

Mrs D. Bibby
Rugby

WHEN buying a camera, always buy a second one so that if you sell the first you will be able to take a picture of it for advertising purposes.

A. Harmer
Frodsham

TAKE your dustbin to the supermarket with you so that you can see which items you have recently run out of.

S. Elliot
London

HELP blind people in the post office by licking their stamps for them. Or better still, teach their dogs to do so.

Mr Beakey
Byker

NEXT time you pop out to the supermarket glue carpet tiles to the soles of your shoes. They'll make Sainsburys feel like your own living room.

D.P.
Bath

TAKE a tip from bank robbers. Leave your engine running when going into a shop to buy frozen vegetables. Making a 'quick get-away' will reduce the risk of them thawing before you get home.

Mrs G. Walton
Holmfirth

ALWAYS use the 'five items or less' checkout at your local supermarket, no matter how many items you have in your trolley. Simply bring a group of friends shopping with you, and divide the contents of your trolley amongst them.

T. Parsnip
Bolhamchesterton-
poolwood

TAKE a leaking tin of red paint to your local D.I.Y. superstore, carry it into the shop and demand a refund. Then return straight to your car in the crowded car park by simply following the trail of paint.

> R. Hiles
> Edinburgh

MAKE shopkeepers feel like criminals and con men by carefully checking **their** change, and holding bank notes up to the light before accepting them.

> Alan Dodsworth
> Leicester

ASK your butcher to thinly slice those old Wellington boots, and hey presto! An endless supply of windscreen wiper blades.

> D. N.
> Farnborough

SAVE on charity donations by spending a pound on clothes at a charity shop, then selling them for 50p to another charity shop. This way you can give twice as much, at half the cost. I think.

> Mrs A. Parker
> Notts.

ALWAYS divide the number of pages in a book by the price to see whether or not it represents good value for money. Compare different books before deciding which to buy.

> L. Flashing
> Andover

IF you get to the supermarket checkout only to find that you have left your purse at home, avoid embarrassment by pretending to have a nose bleed. Inevitably one of the assistants will help you to the lavatory where you can remain until the store has closed.

> Mrs F. Anglia
> Anglia

NEVER attempt to fasten your shoe laces in a revolving supermarket door.

Mr M. Adeye
Plumstead Infirmary

FOOL distant corner shop owners into thinking that you live nearby simply by driving for miles to make frequent early morning and late evening visits to their shop to buy cigarettes, milk, bread and other groceries.

M. Renshaw
London

ANTIQUE shop owners. Calculate the age of old tables by sawing off one of the legs and counting the number of rings in the woodgrain. This works for chairs too.

A. Sapling
Sevenoaks

KEEP kiddies amused on shopping trips by giving them three wooden balls each and offering a goldfish to the first one who can knock a passer-by's hat off.

Hapag Lloyd
Runcorn

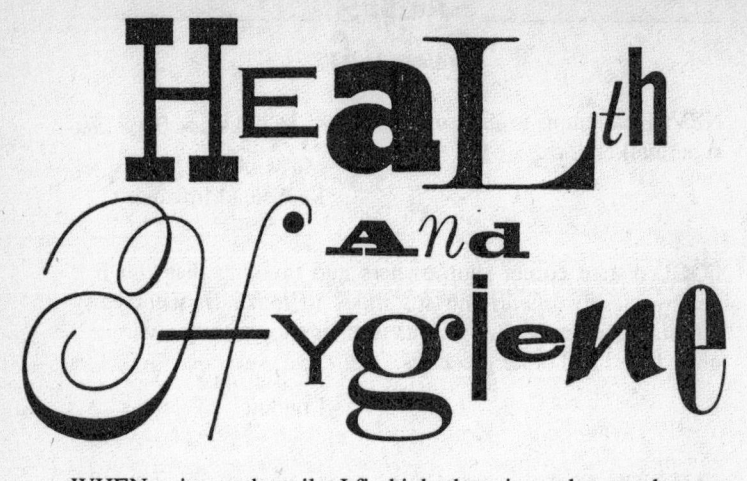

HeaLth and Hygiene

WHEN going to the toilet I find it both easier and more pleasant if I remove both my trousers and my underpants before sitting down.

F. Carruthers
Derby

AT the end of a hard day I find that lying horizontally on a mattress with the lights switched off provides an ideal opportunity for sleep.

A. Caplan
Manchester

LOSE weight quickly by eating raw pork or rancid tuna. I found that the subsequent food poisoning/diarrhoea enabled me to lose 12 pounds in only two days.

K. Dellassus
Newcastle

IF YOU foul the air in someone else's bathroom disguise the smell by lighting a match and setting fire to the hand towel.

Mrs D. Parkinson
Billericay

ON hot summer nights keep cool in bed by using a hot water bottle filled with liquid nitrogen.

Howard Snowplough
Cambridge

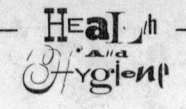
NO TIME for a bath? Wrap yourself in masking tape and remove the dirt by simply peeling it off.

> Dennis Phipps
> Blackburn

I HAVE always found it helpful to unfasten the zip at the front of my trousers before urinating.

> R. Head
> Durham

LIKE a lot of your readers my wife and I enjoy wearing rubber during sexual intercourse. To prevent chafing we always cover ourselves liberally in baking powder. This also helps me 'rise' to the occasion.

> S. Dulay
> Middlesex

IF a small child is choking on an ice cube, don't panic. Make the child drink as many hot drinks as possible, such as tea or coffee, and within minutes the blockage will have simply melted away.

> Mrs F. Kippling
> Swansea

CAN'T afford contact lenses? Simply cut out small circles of 'Cling Film' using a paper punch and then press them onto your eyes.

> D. Stokes
> Middlesex

SLIMMERS. Use sand in coffee instead of sugar. Not only is it free, and contains no calories, but it can also be used more than once, as it doesn't dissolve.

> P. Crocker
> Devon

I SEW figs into the turn-ups of my husband's trousers and in forty years he has never had piles.

> Mrs T. Yorath
> Carlisle

RIGHT-HANDED people. Perform everyday tasks with your left hand, so that if you get a splinter you'll be able to carefully remove it with your right hand.

> A. Pryde
> Bromley

I SLEEP with my house key under my tongue, and I never suffer from cramp.

> Mrs T. Yorath
> Carlisle

ELASTIC bands with a dab of toothpaste make an economical replacement for chewing gum, and are better for your teeth.

> K. Barker
> Barrow-in-Furness

AVOID waiting for a doctor's appointment by making one for 9.00am every morning. If you wake up feeling well, simply phone up and cancel it.

> R. Dury
> Ruddington

EXPENSIVE hair gels are a con. Marmalade is a much cheaper alternative, but beware of bees in the summer.

> M. Boyle
> Surrey

WHENEVER you're shot in the chest, lie on the side you were hit. That way only one lung will fill with blood.

> Major G. Symonds
> Codsall

BY simply fixing a mirror to the ceiling it is possible to examine your feet without looking down.

> L. C. Anderson
> Paris

BRIGHTEN up dull Monday mornings at work by concealing a bottle of vodka in your jacket pocket and taking swigs from it at regular intervals throughout the day.

T. Horswill
Bedford

GIVE friends the impression that you wear contact lenses by blinking frequently midway through conversations, and stopping to carefully pull at your lower eyelids.

Michael Hudson
Bingley

WHILST dieting I used to weigh myself each week. The difference between successive weights was the amount that I had either gained or lost.

A. J. Marsh
Tongham, Surrey

MAKE visits to the dentists less nerve-wracking by popping into the pub first for five or six pints of beer.

T. Horswill
Bedford

PREVENT your cold from spreading by placing a stout paper bag over your head. When you're finished with it, get rid of germs by spraying inside the bag with fly killer. The bag can then be re-used.

S. Evans
Ruddington

ENSURE a good night's sleep by knocking back a large bottle of gin before retiring to bed.

T. Horswill
Bedford

OBTAIN the effect of having a bald, yellow scalp by removing the skin from a bowl of custard and placing it on your scalp.

I. Vandyke
Lancashire

AVOID losing contact lenses by drilling a small hole in each one and attaching them with a length of nylon fishing line. This can then be worn around the neck.

B. Morgan
Criccieth

MAKE everyone think you wear glasses by making a mark on the bridge of your nose with a hot teaspoon every morning.

Morris Minor
Coventry

CUT your man's hair around a mousse ring mould instead of a pudding bowl if he is balding at the crown.

Mrs C. Sidiros
Greenford

SAVE time and hot water in the mornings by simply popping your cold, damp facecloth into the microwave.

P. Wilson
Troon

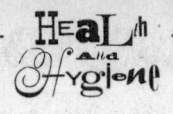
CLAP your hands whilst having a shower. This will help to spray the water in all directions.

Chris Elvin
Japan

WIG wearers. Secure your toupee in high winds by wearing a brightly coloured party hat with elasticated chin strap. Carry a balloon and a bottle of wine, and you'll pass off as an innocent party-goer.

F. Fine-Fare
Fulchester

SILENCE your windy bottom by pulling apart your buttocks before you pump. Hey presto! No embarrassing 'fart' noise.

P. Fletcher
Wrexham

DON'T buy expensive 'ribbed' condoms, just buy an ordinary one and slip a handful of frozen peas inside it before you put it on.

D. Duckham
Didford

EXTERIOR wood stain is a fast, long-lasting and attractive alternative to sun-bed treatments.

Mr T. Eebly
Wanstead

AVOID soiling your trousers by **not** pulling apart your buttocks when you *think* you are about to fart.

P. Fletcher
Wrexham

FAT people. Keep your hands warm in winter by unbuttoning your shirt and tucking them in between the rolling layers of fat on your belly.

M. Jackson
Wolverhampton

LOOK like a super fit body builder by buying a vest that's too small for you and walking around pretending that you've got a roll of carpet under each arm.

Hapag Lloyd
Runcorn

GET RID of irritating pieces of meat stuck between your teeth by popping a handful of maggots into your mouth and allowing them to crawl around your gums for a few minutes after each meal.

I. Meatgone
Nottingham

GIRLS. When applying cosmetics in a mirror place a second mirror on a table behind you. Look over your shoulder in the first mirror to see yourself reflected in the second mirror in order to see what your make-up will actually look like to others, rather than the usual reversed image which you see in a single mirror.

J. Sulzer
Ipswich

GIRLS. Make sure you don't miss out on a tan this summer. Go topless at the first hint of sunshine.

Rob Walker
Harrow

PENSIONERS. Don't forget to retire to bed before 8.00pm so that you can get up tomorrow at the crack of dawn and go and collect your morning paper while anyone with any sense is still sound asleep in bed.

D. Lynch
Quatar

APPLY red nail varnish to fingernails before clipping them. The red nails will be much easier to spot on your bathroom carpet. (Unless you have a red carpet, in which case a contrasting varnish should be selected).

K. Parks
North Chittagong

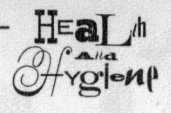

ANOREXICS. When your knees become fatter than your legs, start eating cakes again.

P. Loft
Gateshead

ALWAYS keep tubes of haemorrhoid ointment and Deep Heat rub well separated in your bathroom cabinet.

P. Turner
Liverpool

FATTIES. Pay someone to walk behind you, juggling, swallowing swords or eating fire, etc. This will divert attention from your obesity.

R. Warren
Teddington

FaSHion aND Clothing

GIRLS! A pair of variety size cornflakes packets are ideal for putting fashionable padded shoulders in your blouse.

Mrs. F. Kitching
Southampton

AVOID getting fluff caught in your turn-ups by turning them down. Having done so the fluff will invariable gather elsewhere.

Z. Monkhouse
Gosforth

MUMS! Underpants with legs sewn up make very good hats. Our teenage daughter must be the envy of all her friends at school wearing a pair which my husband disguarded several years ago.

Mrs B.
London

IF you have an artificial leg make it unnoticeable by wearing long trousers.

O. Craig
Stonehaven

STYLISH mirrored sunglasses can be made using two milk bottle tops and some pipe cleaners, saving pounds on similar items sold in trendy shops.

Rick Glover
Malaysia

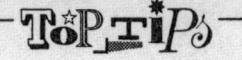

JOIN together hundreds of paper clips to make yourself an attractive 'chain mail' tank top, ideal for a 'knight' out.

> Paul Harvey
> Ash Green

DON'T change your trousers simply because the pockets are full. Add extra pockets by suspending old socks from the belt loops.

> V. Woodsford
> Nottingham

DON'T throw out old balloons after Christmas. Stretched over your head they make perfect shower caps.

> Mrs. D. Topping
> Derby

SAVE money by taking the stitching out of old clothing and using it again.

> G.T.
> Newcastle

INCREASE the weight of your husband's trousers by attaching onions to the belt loops.

> Uncle Len
> Ruddington

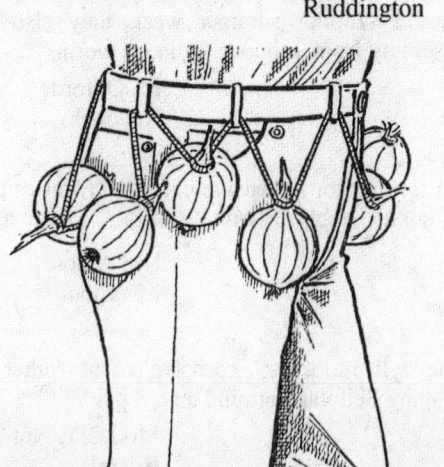

LADIES. Don't splash out on expensive nail files. Make your own by sticking the sides of matchboxes to an old lollipop stick.

Ann Wilson
Preston

ROLL carpet slippers in breadcrumbs, bake until golden brown, then tell friends you're wearing Findus Crispy Pancakes.

H. Lloyd
Runcorn

SMEAR cheap purple dye in your armpits to make people think you've been wearing one of those fantastic, expensive T-shirts that change colour with your body temperature.

Mark Roulston
Swansea

CREATE instant 'designer stubble' in the mornings by rubbing syrup onto your chin and then sprinkling the contents of a tea bag onto it.

B. Measures
Uppingham

BRIGHTLY coloured household slippers are not only comfortable for outdoor summer wear, they also serve to distract passers-by from a toupee, if one is worn.

M. Oxford
Ruddock

WHY pay a fortune for expensive earrings? Mint Imperials or Sugared Almonds, stuck on with 'Blu-Tac', look every bit as good.

Lyn Amos
Liverpool

OBTAIN the stylish looks of expensive patent leather shoes by simply wrapping Sellotape around an old pair.

Mrs. C. P. Nut-Butter
Bristol

SOCIAL
AND
RecREATiONaL

TEAR out the pages of an old book which you have read, shuffle them around and then stick them back together again with Sellotape. Invariably a new story, with unexpected shifts in the plot, emerges.

> D. Portland
> Bognor Regis

SAVE time when listening to LPs by playing them at 45 r.p.m.

> Mrs. D. Phillips
> Bolton

AVOID annoying your neighbours whilst listening to music at full blast by simply disconnecting the speakers from your amplifier.

> P. Hamlet
> Manchester

SWIMMERS. Keep chlorine out of your eyes cheaply but effectively by fashioning a pair of goggles out of two tea bags and an elastic band.

> H. Hill
> Battersea

DON'T sit through rubbish on the TV. When a programme you dislike comes on simply close your eyes and turn down the volume until it has finished.

> J. Drallop
> Bishop Auckland

NOT having a TV I spend my evenings watching a glass fronted cabinet which I pretend is a television. Not only do I save on electricity, but my 'television' does not require a licence.

I.P.A.
Liverpool

I ENJOY drinking socially, but can't afford the expense. So instead of drinking beer I simply gargle it then spit it back into my glass. That way one pint can last me all evening.

Dave Parker
Avon

RATHER than spending a fortune on new gramophone records, try playing old ones at different speeds. Invariably a new 'sound' emerges, with the singer's voice changing somewhat in pitch.

B. West
Blackheath

PUT one inch strips of masking tape across the top and bottom of your TV screen. Then, with the room lights switched off, watch your favourite programmes through binoculars. It's just like being at the cinema.

Mrs. D. Parker
Boddingham

BRIGHTEN up boring snooker on TV by purchasing a sucker tipped dart gun and trying to hit the players on the bottom as they bend down over the table.

A. Foster
Bury

IMPRESS members of the opposite sex by acquiring a comprehensive knowledge of a subject which interests them and then steering the conversation towards this topic.

Paul Armstrong
Manchester

SOciaL
aNd
RecReAtiOnaL

AVOID embarrassing yourself when drunk by taking large quantities of booze to a shed at the bottom of your garden and drinking it all in there.

B and D
Bristol

BY making a simple periscope out of toilet roll tubes and the lenses from an old pair of reflective sunglasses, it is possible to watch your TV from beneath your floorboards.

P. N. Thorne
Bristol

IMPRESS friends by making a list of all the objects in your front room and then inviting them over to play 'I spy'. Watch their faces as you keep winning!

J. Cowell
Milton Keynes

I REGULARLY drive to the pub, but am never guilty of drink driving. The secret is to consume so much alcohol that by closing time you have completely forgotten ever owning a car.

Mike Grey
Essex

BUY a television set exactly like your neighbours. Then annoy them by standing outside their window and changing their channel using you identical remote control.

Leigh Drake
Portsmouth

PUT blue food colouring in your beer next time you visit the pub. Not only is your unusual drink a talking point, but the risk of your pint being stolen while you are at the toilet is greatly reduced.

B. Redesmouth
Hawick

DON'T waste money buying 'Big Country's Greatest Hits' album. Simply buy one of their singles and play it over and over again.

> Paul Goss
> Basildon

SAVE even more money by not buying a Big Country single, simply listen to the theme from BBC TV's 'Z Cars' instead.

> P. Goss
> Basildon

CRICKET spectators. Take a tip from Barry Manilow fans. Strike a match every time a run is scored. When the game is over simply count the number of used matches to reveal the final score.

> Mr U. Biscuits
> Rotherham

SPECTACLE wearers. Avoid the nuisance of low flying military aircraft by sticking strips of brown parcel tape across the top half of your lenses.

> J. Lofts
> Chiswick

CONVINCE people you are the new Messiah by taking a bottle of mineral water into the off license and exchanging it for some cheap wine, buying a loaf of bread and some fish fingers at the corner shop, then getting your mates to nail you to a tree.

> S. G.
> Wembley

PASS off as Welsh by putting coal dust behind your fingernails and talking gibberish all the time, stopping occasionally to sing loudly, or set fire to someone else's house.

> Mr P. Lilburn
> Rotherham

GET into the cinema free of charge by looking bored, carrying an ice cream tray and wearing a silly hat.

> Mrs D. Table
> Hendon

CAN'T afford a video? Lie a toaster sideways on the floor beneath your television. Friends will never know the difference.

> S. Winstanley
> Orrel

AVOID bickering and petty arguments by immediately punching anyone with whom you disagree.

> S. Taylor
> Watford

SPEED up darts games by attaching a length of string to each dart. After throwing, a sharp tug on the string will return your darts to you.

> Patrick Matthews
> Bolton

MAKE people think you have an expensive car phone by calling them, asking them to repeat everything they say, then hanging up half-way through their reply.

> Mr I. Baxter
> Exemouth

TAKE a roll of 'Clingfilm' to the pub. When it's your round use it to cover the tops of the drinks, then carry them back from the bar in your pockets.

> D. Porchester
> Rochester

AVOID the frustration of repeatedly losing your TV remote control by keeping it in a 'cowboy' style holster fashioned out of a child's sock and an old belt.

> M. Thornton
> Jesmond

SPECTACLE wearers. Enjoy foreign language films without the bothersome subtitles by sticking a strip of brown parcel tape across the lower half of your lenses.

J. Lofts
Chiswick

IMPRESS girls this summer by driving up and down the seafront with an ironing board strapped to the roof of your car, and Beach Boys music playing loudly on your cassette player.

B. Meredith
Swansea

STICKING two black circles in the top corners of your TV screen makes the newsreaders look like Mickey Mouse.

S. Teardrop
Teddlebranbuds

FELLAS. Next time you're contemplating masturbation in your bedroom, make sure your bedside lamp is **between** you and the curtains, to avoid giving neighbours and passers-by an entertaining 'shadow play'.

J. Holden
Swindon

FELLAS. Keep wives and girlfriends on their toes by murmuring the names of other women whilst pretending to be asleep.

R. J. Gillon
Coventry

SAVE on booze by drinking cold tea instead of whisky. The following morning you can create the effects of a hangover by drinking a thimble full of washing-up liquid and banging your head repeatedly on a wall.

F. Horton
Chipping Norton

MAKE sex with your wife more exciting by telling her to wear lots of lipstick, and wash her mouth out with vodka. Then you can pretend you're shagging some old scrubber you've just picked up in a nightclub.

F. Lair
Kelso

TV viewers. Avoid laziness by screwing your TV remote control to a wall or a piece of furniture at least ten feet away from your chair.

Hapag Lloyd
Runcorn

OFFICE managers. Encourage primeval 'hunter gathering' instincts among your staff by hiding nuts and berries around the office and encouraging staff to 'forage' for their food at lunch time.

R. Villa
Argentina

RECORD the sound of your wife having an orgasm, and then listen to the tape through headphones next time you make love. That way you can have sex without waking her up.

Frank Wilson
Southend

FELLAS. Avoid pulling ugly birds. Simply drink 14 pints of beer and hey presto! Everyone you chat up looks like Catherine Zeta Jones.

Paul & Scotty
BFPO 544 DRS

MAKE sure she's still a stunner the next morning by hiding a bottle of vodka under your pillow, and drinking it before she wakes up. Hey presto! Breakfast with Cindy Crawford.

Paul & Scotty
BFPO 544 DRS

PRETEND you're listening to Radio One on long wave by slightly off tuning the FM frequency and then wrapping the radio in a sleeping bag.

H. Clayton
Gateshead

STEREO too loud? Simply place the speakers inside a cupboard. The volume can then be easily controlled by opening and closing the cupboard doors.

L. Shufflebottom
Market Drayton

GET the feel of camping outdoors without the inconvenience by turning off your heating, releasing ants on your bedroom carpet, crapping on the floor, then sleeping on it, wrapped in a plastic bin liner.

Graeme Marsh
Ashford

DROP a table tennis ball into public urinals and invite other toilet users to play 'piss tennis' by directing the ball backwards and forwards along the urinal with your wees.

J. Naylor
Northwich

ENCOURAGE friends to telephone you by offering a free plastic dinosaur for every call you receive.

Hapag Lloyd
Runcorn

FELLAS. Play 'Rodeo Sex' by shagging your missus 'doggy fashion' and then calling her another bird's name. See how long you can stay on for!

Karin Love
Nottingham

WHEN photographing windmills attach a white handerkchief to the end of one of the sails. When your picture is developed this will prove invaluable in indicating both wind direction and sail rotation.

R. Well
Holland

RAMBLERS. In the countryside leaving gates **open** will help the farmer, as he will not have to climb down from his tractor.

W. A. Pratt
London

FELLAS. Why waste money on expensive '0898' phone numbers. Just phone your local department store, tell them its your wife's birthday, and ask them to describe their latest selection of ladies' lingerie (while you masturbate furiously).

A. Jax
Wolverhampton

RE-KINDLE memories of your summer holiday in sunny Greece by turning off your water supply, removing all toilet roll from your bathroom, placing a dirty bucket next to your toilet and forcing some Plasticine up behind your index finger nail.

Richard B.
Thurrock

RE-CREATE the fairground thrills of the 'Waltzer' in your own home by simply drinking 12 cans of Carlsberg Special Brew then asking a couple of friends to stand at the end of your bed and occasionally give it a violent shove as you try to get to sleep.

S. Leone
Moffat

A SWISH curtain rail, a pyjama cord and a hat pin provide a cheap but effective bow and arrow for Robin Hood games in the park. Alternatively, in these safety conscious times, why not substitute a sink plunger for the hat pin?

Mrs D. Treliss
Colwyn Bay

FELLAS. Next time you have to wrap up a present, don't, because you're shite at it. Give it to the wife and she'll do it properly with extra girlie bows and fiddly bits while you're down the pub.

Daphnie Treloar
Cardiff

NON-SWIMMERS. Fill a pair of goggles with water and put them on. Then dip your nose in a cup of water, and squirt water into both your ears with a water pistol. Hey presto! You're experiencing all the pleasures of swimming without the inconvenience or expense of travelling to your local pool.

Andrew Powell
Portsmouth

GOLFERS. Why waste a fortune on expensive covers for the heads of your golf clubs. An empty crisp packet will do the job just as well. Use different flavours for different clubs, e.g. cheese'n'onion – three iron, salt'n'vinegar – sand wedge, etc.

A. Simmons
Cheltenham

GIRLS. Next time you feel like throwing a ball over-arm, don't do it, because you can't and it just looks silly. Just throw it girlie under-arm style, and no-one will laugh at you, or get hurt.

> D. Thresher
> Wapping

GOLFERS. Empty egg cartons make ideal containers for your golf balls. Except that they are a little bit too small.

> A. Simmons
> Cheltenham

FOR those who haven't got enough money for two weeks holiday, go for one week and don't go to bed.

> Christopher 'Monty'
> Heading .
> Aged 8. Nottingham

GOLFERS. An ice cream cornet makes an ideal golf tee for use in emergencies.

> A. Simmons
> Cheltenham

HouseHold Hints 2

TEENAGERS. Fed up with posters falling off the wall? Simply file them in a filing cabinet under 'P' and you'll know exactly where to find them if you want a quick look.

John Kean
Sheffield

SAVE money on doorbell batteries by removing them and simply popping to the door every two minutes to see if anyone is there.

Rod Scott
Leicester

FUMES from burning settees can be lethal so before sitting down always look around and plan your escape route in the event of a fire.

D. Purnell
Bristol

DISPOSE of used toilet roll tubes in threes. Two can be compressed and then inserted into the other one to save space in the rubbish bin.

Mrs D. Park
Bedlington

PILE bricks at one end of your bath and it will require much less hot water to fill it up.

James Lowe
Nottingham

SAVE electricity by turning off all the lights in your house and walking around wearing a miner's hat.

D. Purvis
Bolton

LADIES. A toilet freshener in your handbag helps keep it smelling fresh.

Jackie P.
Bolton

CUT laundry bills. Tie your dirty linen to your neighbour's roof rack next time he visits the car wash.

R. Hughes
Mid Glamorgan

SINCE our daughter outgrew her potty we have used it as an attractive fruit bowl, a far cheaper alternative to the expensive fruit bowls which you see in the shops nowadays.

J. Moy
Hull

OLD folks. Avoid confusion between these new 'microwave' ovens and televisions by cutting out a large letter 'M' in brightly coloured paper, and sticking it to the door of the oven.

Mrs G. Jones
Leicester

WHO needs a dish washer? Simply arrange your dirty dishes on your next door neighbour's roof rack the next time he goes to the car wash.

R. Hughes
Mid Glamorgan

DON'T waste money on these expensive 'binoculars'. Simply stand closer to the object you wish to see.

S. Goldhanger
Fulchester

MAKE cheap but effective baby rattles by gluing a lollipop stick to an empty matchbox, then filling it with ten woodlice.

Ms. G. M. Dowd
Wigan

MAKE bathtime as much fun for kiddies as a trip to the seaside, by chucking a bucket of sand, a bag of salt, a dog turd and a broken bottle into the bath with them.

Archie Hitch
Merton

SAVE constant wear and tear on door hinges by only opening doors a little bit, and then squeezing through the gap.

Dino
Eastleigh

TO avoid losing keys, every time you put them down ring a friend and tell him where you put them. Later, if you can't find them, simply ring your friend and ask him where they are.

Peter Evans
Bristol

REMOVE pocket fluff from boiled sweets by filing them gently with the edge of a matchbox.

H. Osborne
Colchester

OLD telephone directories make ideal personal address books. Simply cross out the names and address of people you don't know.

Mrs K. Smith
Bristol

TAKE a 'Thermos' flask to bed instead of a hot water bottle. The water stays hot much longer, and you can use it to make a cup of tea in the morning.

S.T.W.
Bristol

HELP forget the farce that was Prince Andrew's marriage by sticking the head of your favourite film actress over Fergie's head on any souvenirs you have around the house. I now have an attractive portrait of Prince Andrew with Hollywood stunner Michelle Pfeiffer on my mantlepiece.

Mrs Dawn Potts
Cheltenham

KEEP losing the end of the Sellotape? Then why not coat it in sugar? When you need to use it simply lick off the sugar, use the tape, and then re-coat the new end.

G. Davis
Herts.

THREAD a long length of string through everything that you have in your home. Whenever you misplace something, simply follow the string from beginning to end and eventually you'll come across the missing item.

E. Tupp
Glamorgan

CONVINCE friends and neighbours that you have a high powered job in the City by leaving for work at 6am every morning, arriving home at 10 at night, never keeping social appointments, and dropping down dead at the age of 36.

S. James
Barnes

ENSURE circular objects such as vases stand centrally on your mantlepiece by subtracting the diameter of the object from the length of the mantlepiece and dividing by two. Then simply cut a piece of string to that length. Get a friend to hold one end of the string flush to one side of the mantlepiece, and then slide the vase or object along the length of the string towards the centre of the mantlepiece. Stop only when the string runs out, and its other end abuts the base of the vase or object. The string can then be popped into the vase, and used again later should the ornament be moved for any reason.

M. Moleson
Wadebridge

DON'T throw away old pieces of string simply because they're too short. Knot them together and hey presto! A new, longer, useful piece of string.

Sam Evans
Shropshire

INCREASE the life of your carpets by rolling them up and keeping them in the garage.

A. Allied
South Wales

FIND your way to the toilet in the dark by tying a length of string from the toilet bowl to the toilet door handle. Simply straddle the string and slide the cleft of your buttocks along it until you feel the toilet seat touch your genitals. Simple.

S. Jeames
Brighton

USING string, nails and pulleys it is possible to turn on your hot water tap in the bathroom from the bedroom. By the time you walk to the bathroom the water will have warmed up.

E. Barnpot
Devon

KEEP a hammer close to your bed in case any nails fall out of the ceiling at night.

Nick Dwyer
Brighton

WHY waste money on first class stamps? Simply write your letters a few days earlier, and send them second class.

P. Honk
Leamington Spa

SAVE on expensive washing powder by stealing your neighbours' clean washing from their line.

E. K. Wright
Ashington

STOP visitors from using your phone without asking by taking it off the hook, and sitting on the receiver.

Nick Dwyer
Brighton

STRETCH a piece of elastic and make marks at one inch intervals. Hey presto! A telescopic ruler which takes up little room in a handbag or pocket. By stretching it to different degrees you can easily convert it from imperial to metric measurements.

A. Kinloch
Harringay

AVOID burns from a hot iron by placing the garment over a hot ring on the electric cooker, and then rubbing it with a cold iron.

M. T.
Greenwich

A SIMPLE plant pot, upturned on the top of your head, is ideal for doing comedy impressions of the late Tommy Cooper. Just like that!

R. Alderson
Nantwich

MAKE guests believe your house may be bugged by running your hands under tables and inside lamp shades and turning on the shower every time you want to speak.

C. Rumple
Balham

WHEN packing expensive objects in a box popcorn makes an ideal replacement for expensive polystyrene 'chips'.

Mr Edwards
Leighton Buzzard

DON'T throw away those old car batteries. Placed inside an old pillow case they make an ideal counter balance on a see-saw.

Alex
Burnley

CAN'T find a dictionary? Ever thought of trying a telephone directory? They contain many useful words, like Cooper, Black and Smart, all of which are listed in alphabetical order.

R. Clayton
Arbroath

FOOL next door neighbours into thinking you have more stairs than them by banging your feet **twice** on each stair.

C. B.
Sedgefield

OLD contact lenses make ideal 'portholes' for small model boats.

F. Johnson
Seaham

BATTENBURG cake, cut into 16 slices then arranged into a square, makes an ideal emergency chess board.

Graham Carter
Ashford, Middlesex

IF you feel someone is taking an unreasonable length of time to answer the phone, punish them by putting the receiver down the second they eventually answer.

Ben Collins
Sunderland

WHY pay the earth for expensive jigsaws? Just take a bag of frozen chips from the freezer and try piecing together potatoes.

B. Reastford
Ironville, Notts.

MAKE neighbours think you have Norwegian visitors staying by leaving whale bones outside your back door along with your rubbish.

E. M.
North Shields

KEEP a few ten pence pieces in your pyjama pocket in case you are abducted by aliens during the night and need to 'phone home'.

H. Lord
Redcar

MARRIED couples. Avoid damage to doors by attaching a balloon to the top of the door frame before starting a row. When you storm out of the room at the height of the row closing the door gently will have the same dramatic effect as a violent slam, without causing any damage to the door.

O. Stacey
Essex

HI-FI enthusiasts. Clean the inside of your CD player by washing your CDs in hot, sudsy water and then playing them immediately on full volume. As they spin the water will be sprayed throughout the CD console. Repeat with cold water to rinse.

Chip Rowe
Washington DC, USA

PRETEND to live in a hard water area by placing finely ground pieces of egg shell in the bottom of your kettle.

A. J. Hill
Grantham

PENSIONERS. Save on heating bills this winter by recalling the moment, at the 1992 pre-election Labour Party Rally, when Neil Kinnock said: "Comrades. Alright! Alright! Well **alright!**" The thought of it will make you glow from head to foot with embarrassment.

D. T.
Cardiff

WHEN throwing someone a sharp instrument such as a Stanley knife, or bread knife, always throw it blade first as they invariably tend to turn whilst in the air.

W. Stannier
Cricklewood

FIND out what you look like when you're asleep by learning 'astral projection', and then glancing over your shoulder just as you are leaving your body.

Steve Wright
Hornsey

DON'T fork out on expensive smoke alarms. Simply fill balloons with water and hang them from the ceiling. Then cover the floor with air-filled balloons, each with a drawing pin stuck to the top. In the event of a fire the temperature will cause the air-filled balloons to rise up from the floor, and the pins will burst the water-filled balloons, thus extinguishing the fire. Probably.

D. P.
Wiltshire

SAVE the cost of installing cable TV by taping current editions of Top Of The Pops and then watching them in fifteen years' time.

Lex Mouzer
Liverpool

AN even sprinkling of flour will lighten up the colour of your carpet. If you don't like the new shade, no problem. Simply vacuum if off.

C. Jones
Reading

REMOVE all buttons from articles of clothing before you place them in the washing machine. This will prevent the buttons from making a 'clanking' sound when they bang against the glass in the washing machine door.

Mrs I. Graham
Berkshire

REMOVE the laces from any odd boots and shoes which you find washed up on the beach. Pop them inside a sock next time you wash any clothes, then dry them with an iron and keep them in an old yoghurt carton for use as spares.

A. Houndog
Cumbria

READ small print easily and without the use of expensive glasses by looking at it through a pint glass full of water.

E. C.
Leeds

BOMB disposal experts' wives. Keep hubby on his toes by packing his lunchbox with plasticine and an old alarm clock.

E. F.
Chester-le-Street

WHY waste money on expensive answering machines? When you leave the house simply plug your phone into the video recorder. Not only will it record the caller's voice, but you'll also get a TV picture of them speaking. Probably.

T. J. Jones
Valenton

AniMals and PETs

PREVENT your dog from feeling left out at breakfast time by feeding him dog food out of a 'variety' size Cornflakes packet.

D. Purnell
Bristol

WHEN they die embalm household pets and seal them in plastic to make perfect draught excluders. It's nice to know that your much loved pets are still with you around the house, helping to keep you warm on cold winter nights.

Mrs L. Eptons
Birkenhead

ONE or two days before moving house place your goldfish bowl in the ice-making compartment of your refrigerator. When the time comes to move you will find that your fish can be transported in a car or van with no danger of spillage.

Mr D. A. Roberts
Hillingdon

STOP birds nesting in your garden by collecting all the twigs and moss in your neighbourhood and hiding it in your garden shed.

P. Reaney
Rothwell

AVOID the unnecessary expense of buying clay pigeons by shooting real ones.

A. Smith
Rosyth

A SMALL hole cut out of a window will allow your budgie to come and go as it pleases.

C. Press
Manchester

STOP squirrels and birds taking food from your bird table by placing the food inside a biscuit tin, and securing the lid with heavy duty tape.

P. Reaney
Rothwell

PUTTING just the right amount of gin in your goldfish bowl makes the fishes' eyes bulge and causes them to swim in an amusing manner.

Magnus McIntyre
Oxford

PREVENT bees and butterflies stealing your pollen by enclosing each flower head in a plastic bag securely fastened around the stem with a clothes peg.

P. Reaney
Rothwell

IF a dog is about to attack you in the street, stand your ground. Do not show any sign of fear, as this would encourage the animal to attack.

Mrs B. Sellers
Cricklewood

DETER your canary from flying around its cage by placing bulldog clips on both of its wings.

M. Faraday
Barking

Tᴼᴾᵀⁱᴾ₅

PLACE dead goldfish inside library books and slam the books shut. The squashed fish will serve as useful bookmarks, and are doubly handy as their smell will act as a reminder that the books are due for return.

Doris Franklin
Weymouth

IF being pursued by a rogue rhinoceros run in a straight line directly away from the animal. Just before he catches you, dart quickly to one side or the other. Unable to stop or change direction, the bulky animal's momentum will carry him a good distance away, enabling you to run up a tree and call for help.

Mrs B. Sellers
Cricklewood

A CORK dangling from the end of a long stick can be used to chase flies harmlessly out of the window.

Mrs Doris Peterson
Rhyll

STOP being scared of spiders by handling spiders on a regular basis until you aren't scared of spiders anymore.

Mrs Nan Chester
Manchester

DON'T panic when being chased overland by a crocodile. Simply run in a zig-zag fashion. These large reptiles are only able to run in straight lines and will be confused by your constant changes in direction. Soon he will give up the chase.

Mrs B. Sellers
Cricklewood

CAT owners. Convince neighbours that you own a racing cat by putting a dish cloth over its back, wearing binoculars round your neck, and leading it in circles around your lawn.

Mrs Wm. Holland
Stanton-in-Leak

WHEN attacked by a large polar bear, roll into a ball and remain perfectly still. Any movement on your part will excite the animal and increase your chance of injury.

> Mrs B. Sellers
> Cricklewood

DISAPPOINT wasps this summer by smearing cold tea on your ears instead of honey.

> T. Shankborne
> Coventry

HOUSEWIVES. Throw a fish carcass into a bucket of cement, and hey presto! You have an instant fossil.

> Tam Dale
> Glasgow

REVIVE dying moths by placing them on a small droplet of sugary water.

> C. Coup
> Basildon

ADD an element of danger to your gerbil's boring life by hiding a bowl of Ready Brek under its sawdust with a small sign nearby saying 'Danger – quicksand'.

> Hapag Lloyd
> Runcorn

A BUCKET of water hung in a tree is an ideal nesting place for migrating sea birds.

H. Lovatt
Reading

MIX luminous paint with your dog food to help prevent unfortunate pedestrians treading in dog mess during the dark winter evenings.

Simon Mellishoe
Redhill

SCABS with tufts of fur attached removed from your cat make ideal fishing flies.

D.T.
Cardiff

VICARS. Raise much-needed restoration funds by inviting the owners of lost pets to climb to the top of your steeple in order to look for their missing animals, in return for a small donation.

B. O. Nails
Nantwich

DOG owners. Next time your dog does a 'soft one' on the beach annoy metal detector owners by dropping nuts and bolts into it and then covering it with sand.

L. O'Hara
Inverness

SEAGULLS. Fly upside down next time you're over Cornwall. I can assure you it isn't even worth shitting on.

I. Ashenden
Falmouth

VIDEO your goldfish swimming in its bowl, then place your TV set next to the bowl, and play back the tape. Hey presto! Instant 'company' for your fish. Duplicate the tape and use extra televisions to create a 'goldfish party' for special occasions.

Mrs B. Lane
Aston Clinton, Bucks.

UNDERWATER cameramen. Don't throw away those old discarded supermarket trolleys. Tied together with string two of them make a handy anti shark cage.

Hapag Lloyd
Runcorn

NAIL old floorboards to your tree in order to attract woodpeckers.

Robin Pearce
Southampton

GIVE your goldfish a love-bite by inserting a straw into its bowl and sucking gently at its neck.

W. B. Levit
Hull

MAKE neighbours think they've seen a snake by squirming around on their lawn in a rolled-up carpet with a fork dangling from your mouth, and making hissing noises.

Tam Dale
Glasgow

CONVERT black labrador dogs into seals by feeding them pastries, sweets and cakes, starving them of exercise, slipping a pair of black socks onto their front paws and smearing their coats in vaseline. Then encourage them to balance a beach ball on their nose in return for fish-shaped dog biscuits.

> R. Crosbie
> Cheltenham

WEIGH your pet by first of all weighing yourself, then weighing yourself again, this time carrying your pet. Deduct the first weight from the second to reveal your pet's weight. (If weighing goldfish, remember to make an allowance for the weight of the bowl and the water).

> Rob Keith
> Nottingham

A LENGTH of drainpipe with a roller skate fastened to each end makes an ideal 'car' for a snake.

> L. Hall
> Morpeth

Christmas & Party Time

A SMALL tree standing in the corner of the room decorated with coloured lights, tinsel and baubles makes an ideal Christmas decoration.

H. Lovatt
Reading

PLACE the candles evenly around the surface of a frozen Birthday cake. Lighting them early will help defrost it in time for your party.

Mrs J. Thomas
Ryegate

RUN out of ice for party drinks? Frozen peas are an ideal replacement, and can always be washed and re-used afterwards.

D. Purnell
Bristol

MUMS! When clearing up after children's parties, always burst balloons before throwing them away. This way you use far fewer dustbin liners.

Mrs M. Smith
Titchfield Common

WHO said used Tampons were useless? A spot of glue and half a tube of glitter transforms them into ideal Christmas tree decorations.

Christine Williams
Wimbledon

AN IDEAL yet inexpensive Christmas gift for the smoker is a novelty cigarette lighter made from an ordinary house brick with a match tied onto it with a piece of string.

David Parkinson
Banbury

PLACE your Christmas tree in an alcove, bay window or similar recess. After Christmas block it off using empty Cornflakes packets to form a partition wall. Come next December simply pull down the wall, and hey presto! There's your tree, decorations and all.

B. Carpenter
Huddersfield

At party time Cornflakes packets make ideal jelly moulds for anyone requiring large rectangular blocks of jelly. Although they do have the disadvantage of not being waterproof.

Mrs E. Norris
Bath

NEXT time you have a party make all the guests swallow a small plastic disc with a number on it, making sure to keep a record. If anyone vomits, you'll know who it was.

Innes Reid
Bangor

CAN'T play the piano? Then why not entertain party guests with a comical impression of snooker star Dennis Taylor, by simply wearing your glasses upside down.

B. Potter
Aberdeen

AT party time put food colouring in guests' drinks, a different colour for each guest. Not only will the colours brighten up your party, but if anyone urinates on the bathroom floor you'll know who it was.

Innes Reid
Bangor

A STRING of sausages draped across the room makes an ideal edible Christmas decoration. But be sure to cook them before giving them to the kids.

Mrs I. Jones
Hebden Bridge

SPRINKLE in an inch deep covering of talcum powder over your carpets this Christmas, and encourage your kids to walk around the house barefoot. Not only does it create a wonderful 'snow' effect, it also helps to prevent athletes' foot.

Mrs R. House
Embleton

CONVINCE your postman that you are more popular than you actually are by sending yourself several hundred Christmas cards each year.

T. James
Huddersfield

HANG brussels sprouts on the end of a piece of string. Hey presto! Edible Christmas decorations for the kids.

Mrs I. Jones
Hebden Bridge

PLANNING a kids' party? Remember to make your cactus plants safe for the children by removing all the spines with a pair of tweezers.

Gillian Tasker
Derbyshire

PINEAPPLE rings make attractive tree decorations, and slot easily onto the branches of your tree. Leave the remaining juice in a glass on the mantlepiece – an ideal treat for Santa!

Mrs I. Jones
Hebden Bridge

SAVE pounds at Christmas by not sending cards or presents to elderly relatives whose marbles have probably gone anyway and who wouldn't know you from Adam.

B. Peacock
Swindon

GLUE desiccated coconut to your windows this Christmas for a perfect 'snow' effect. Afterwards it can be chiseled off and fried – a perfect treat for the kids!

Mrs I. Jones
Hebden Bridge

FROZEN sprouts are a tasty alternative to boiled sweets. And they don't rot kids' teeth.

Mrs F. Penn
Burnley

MASHED potato looks a bit like snow, and is harmless for children.

H. Civic
Southampton

DON'T invite drug addicts round for a meal on Boxing Day. They may find the offer of 'cold turkey' embarrassing or offensive.

Steven Howlett
London N8

Odds 'n' Sods

POLICEMEN. Why not walk up and down the street remarking to each other how the public are getting older every day.

D. Tucker
Chelmslow

INTERNATIONAL master criminals. Tell your guards to shoot James Bond in the head at the first available opportunity. Under no circumstances give him a guided tour of your base, or leave him in the custody of attractive women in bikinis.

S. Stars
Welwyn

FAST food restaurant staff. Fill cups with ice before pouring soft drinks, so that customers get only a fraction of what they pay for.

B. King
London

AMERICAN organised crime leaders. Upon capturing the 'A' Team do not under any circumstances lock them in a shed full of tools and useful scrap materials.

Chris Jones
Reading

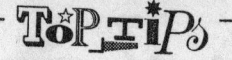

ARCH villians of Gotham City. Should the opportunity present itself kill Batman and Robin using traditional techniques (gun, knife, etc.) rather than leaving them unattended at the mercy of some untested 'Heath Robinson' style killing machine of your own design.

C. Gordon
Gotham City P.D.

STAR Trek security officers. If you have never appeared in the programme before and suddenly Captain Kirk asks you to join a landing party, make an excuse. Under no circumstances should you beam down to the planet surface, as you will invariably be killed.

Mr L. Hall
Northumberland

TELEPHONE salesmen. Increase company profits by reversing the charges whenever you call a customer. Invariably they'll accept the call, thinking it may be a relative in distress.

A. F.
London

BOOKSELLERS. Get rid of unsold piles of Viz 'Top Tips' books by turning them around and displaying them upside down. Hopefully people will then mistake them for the latest sexually revealing autobiography by horny Tory romeo love rat Alan Clark.

J. Brown
The South of France

A new selection of

appears in every issue of

*On sale from newsagents
every two months.*